THE Seine

RIVER OF PARIS

Harbor at Dieppe on the Seine

the SEINE

RIVER of PARIS

by HAZEL WILSON

GARRARD PUBLISHING COMPANY
CHAMPAIGN, ILLINOIS

THIS BOOK WAS EDITED AND DESIGNED
UNDER THE SUPERVISION OF NANCY LARRICK, ED. D.

*For reading the manuscript of this book
and checking the accuracy of its content,
the author and editor are grateful to*

Dr. PIERRE E. BRODIN
Director of Studies, Lycée Français de New-York

Manufactured in the United States of America
Library of Congress Catalog Number: 62-7575

Charles Trieschman from Black Star

Contents

1. *A Small Beginning* 7

2. *The City of Light* 18

3. *The Bridges of Paris* 31

4. *The Two Patron Saints of Paris* 43

5. *Chalk Hills and a Castle* 48

6. *The Hill of the Two Lovers* 57

7. *Factory Chimneys and Church Steeples* 60

8. *On to Le Havre* 70

9. *The Pictured River* 77

10. *The Moving Road* 83

Pronunciation Guide 93

Index 94

1. A Small Beginning

Everybody wants to see Paris. And to see Paris is to make the acquaintance of the river Seine. The Seine and Paris belong more closely together than any other river and city in the world. One does not think of them separately. Together they are Paris, capital of France, home of the Parisians and second home to people from many countries.

Many people know only the eight miles of the Seine within the city limits of Paris. They are the most famous miles. Yet all of its 482 miles from its source to the English Channel have much variety and charm.

People lived along its banks long before the time of Christ. Its calm waters have reflected battles of

7

Map by René Martin

ancient and recent wars. Yet many miles of the Seine have always known peace and quiet, broken only by bird song or the patient movements of fishermen.

The Seine has a personality of its own. It is as different from other rivers as one person's face is from another's.

The Seine begins in a shallow forest pool fed by a spring. It is in that part of the province of Burgundy called the Côte-d'Or. Freely translated, that means the *Golden Hillside*. It is a gently sloping plateau. There are famous vineyards near the Seine's small beginning. Some of the finest French wines are made from grapes grown near by.

Grape picker in Burgundy on the Côte-d'Or.

This statue stands beside the pool where the Seine begins.

A path in the woods leads to the pool where the Seine begins. Beside the pool is a statue of the river nymph, Sequana. This was erected in the year 1867 by the City of Paris. The statue is not the first honor paid the Seine. Near the spring-fed pool are crumbled rocks. They are all that remains of a Roman temple built for the worship of the river goddess. Even the small beginning of the Seine has been known for a long, long time.

From the pool a tiny rivulet starts its long north-westward journey to the sea. For most of the first mile, the stream is so small that a child can jump across it. During a dry summer it may disappear,

9

leaving its bed bare. A heavy rain always revives the tiny stream, and soon other rivulets join and strengthen it.

Not much more than a mile from its source, the stream flows through a long stone building roofed with tiles. Here women come to scrub and rinse their washing. Away from the cities there are still French women who prefer to wash clothes in a river. There are several outdoor laundries along the upper part of the Seine. Sometimes a woman kneels alone on a board in a niche in the river bank. It is her own private laundry.

Every day is washday by the river bank.

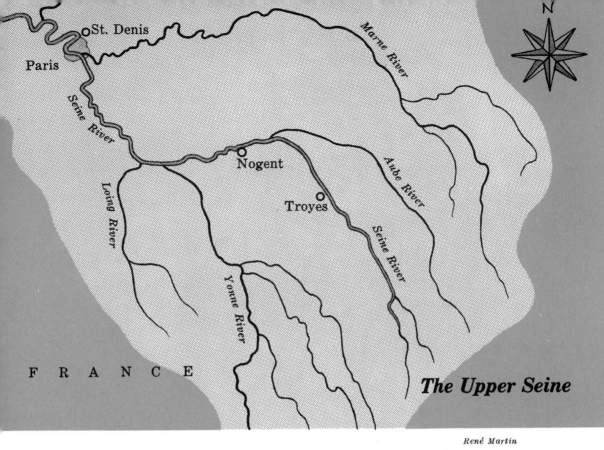

René Martin

From its source, the Seine and its tributaries flow toward Paris.

Clumps of reeds grow along the low river bank. Beyond them are meadows and farm lands. Few cultivated fields reach to the river. This is because the Seine sometimes overflows its banks after heavy spring rains. Yet its floods are usually gentle.

The Seine has less than 1,600 feet to come down in its slow descent to the sea. Since it is nearly 500 miles from the source to the sea, it is in no hurry. It mirrors

11

French Government Tourist Office

Villages along the Seine look like a storybook.

overhanging willows and stiff rows of poplar trees. It has time to reflect trees, stars and clouds.

Here in the country the little river is a pleasant place for children to wade. They launch bark boats and send them down river. Sometimes they run along the bank following their frail toy boats for a while. Boys come to fish from the grassy banks of the stream.

12

A loaded barge moves down river through beautiful country.

Worms and insects or bits of meat are good bait. But some small boys claim that fish bite best on a ripe red cherry.

The crystal clear river Douix pours its waters into the Seine 32 miles from its source. Rowboats have appeared on the river for some miles now. Yet not until the Seine reaches the city of Troyes, is it deep

13

enough for barges. These freight-bearing boats have been going up and down the Seine for centuries. Years ago barges were propelled by sails helped out by oars when there was no breeze. Now some of the barges have gasoline or Diesel engines. Many of them have no engines and are pulled several at a time by tugboats.

At Troyes the river is really made to work. This is a grain and textile center where factory chimneys are seen among the spires of medieval churches. But Troyes is older than the Middle Ages. It has been sending wheat to Paris since the days of the Romans.

When the river Aube joins the Seine below Troyes, the Seine is little no longer. It has become a wide, deep, but slowly moving river. It flows through woods and meadows, past villages and towns. It passes Nogent, famous for eels trapped in the river, and Montereau, where the Yonne River empties into it. It flows on to Saint-Mammès, a sort of depot for barges. Here they take on oil and food supplies for their crews. The water is oil-stained near the piers where barges are moored.

Where the river Yonne joins the Seine.

Down river from the Seine's junction with the Yonne, the landscape is partly rural, partly industrial. Yet there is scarcely a mile where men cannot be seen fishing from the river banks or from rowboats tied to stakes near the shore. There are stretches of carefully tended woods, which look more like parks than forests. Cattle stand in the shade of great oak trees.

15

Restaurant tables are on terraces overlooking the river.

Sometimes the river makes a gentle bend. It is all pleasant countryside of much variety. There is even an occasional small beach of gravel and pebbles. People from Paris drive out to enjoy the riverside before the stream reaches the city.

Just before the Seine becomes part of Paris, the Marne River joins it. Soon after, the Seine makes a great bend within the city. The river is slow and deep, a moving mirror as it flows between stone embank-

Along the Seine every man is a fisherman.

F. S. Lincoln

A long bamboo pole is a favorite fishing rod.

ments. Here the Seine has reached its geographical center, midway between its source and the English Channel.

The Seine has helped make Paris one of the important trade centers of the world. Like a broad silver ribbon in Paris sunshine, it has always adorned the city. Partly because of the beauty of the river, Paris is considered the loveliest city of France if not of all the world.

17

The boat-shaped island is the center of Paris.

2. The City of Light

The first settlement of Paris was on a small island in the Seine. It is shaped like a boat with its bow headed downstream. This island, the Ile de la Cité, is still the center of Paris. Slightly upstream there is a smaller island, the Ile Saint-Louis, which is also part

18

of Paris. But it was on the Ile de la Cité that Paris was born.

The Seine divides so its two arms surround the two islands. Water on each side makes a settlement easy to defend. That was why early tribes settled on the Ile de la Cité. Nobody knows a great deal about these early settlers. But some authorities claim that the name Paris was derived from the name of its earliest inhabitants.

They were conquered by the Romans, who built the first city on the Ile de la Cité. The Roman homes, palaces and temples were built from stone quarried near the banks of the Seine. Because the limestone was so nearly white, the Romans called their city Lutetia, meaning *White City*. Years later the name was changed to Paris.

While still a Roman city, Paris outgrew its island. The city spread first to the left bank of the Seine and then to the right. The ruins of a wall, a Roman bath and the remains of a sports arena are still standing. The Romans established Paris as a center of trade and a highly civilized city. So it has remained.

Seal
of the city
of Paris

For many centuries there have been river traders on the Seine. During the Middle Ages they were organized almost like a labor union of today. Their seal was a picture of a ship with a motto in Latin, *Fluctuat nec mergitur*. That meant that though buffeted by the waves, the ship would never sink.

In time the motto of the river traders became the motto of the City of Paris. It appears on the Paris coat of arms with the outline of a sailing ship. You can see it carved on stone buildings and bridges.

The people of Paris believe in the deeper meaning of the motto. They think of Paris as the ship. They say that although the city may undergo misfortune, it will never be destroyed.

No city has lived through more changes than Paris. After the long rule of the Romans, it was conquered by Germanic tribes. Celts and Franks made the city their home.

Then came the days when fierce Norsemen sailed up to Paris from the coast, looting and burning villages on the way. A Norse leader once accepted a bag of gold as a price for sparing Paris. Some Norse-

People sit for hours in the sidewalk cafés of Paris.

men liked France so well that they did not return to their own country.

The people of Paris, as of all France, are a mixture of many races. The city has been besieged and occupied by enemies. It has known bloody revolutions. But Paris has always recovered. It remains a great and beautiful city.

The Seine divides Paris into two great sections, the Right Bank and the Left Bank. Except on the Ile de la Cité and the Ile Saint-Louis, which are in the river, everything in Paris is on either the Right or the Left Bank of the Seine. New York and other cities have their east side and their west. But in Paris the river is of more importance than the points of the compass.

The Right Bank has most of the great boulevards, the smartest shops and hotels, the art museum, the Louvre, the opera house and the highest point in the city, Montmartre. Much of the Left Bank seems older than the right. Here are the University of Paris and the student quarter. At sidewalk cafés, students and artists eat and drink and argue about life and art. Children sail boats in the pool in the Luxembourg

Right: Black-and-white reproduction of a colorful painting by Utrillo of Sacré-Coeur on Montmartre.

French Government Tourist Office

Gardens. There are old, old churches and the domed Panthéon where famous Frenchmen are buried.

The Eiffel Tower is on the Left Bank. It is a tower of ironwork tapering to a height of 984 feet. From its top you can get a wonderful view of Paris. Far below you see the curving river, its many bridges, the tops of trees like green bouquets and an endless variety of rooftops.

From the Eiffel Tower you get a bird's-eye view of Paris.

The Cathedral of Notre-Dame

Old French engraving from Frederic Lewis

Here is the Ile de la Cité. It seems to be moored to land on each side by bridges. Another bridge links it to the Ile Saint-Louis. One can see the twin gray towers of the Cathedral of Notre-Dame. From the Eiffel Tower you can get an idea of the shape of the city. The plaster-white church of Sacré-Coeur crowns the heights of Montmartre on the Right Bank. The lower hills of Montparnasse are on the Left.

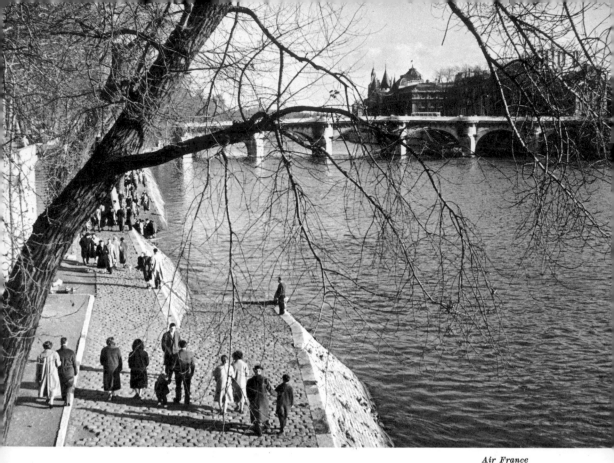

There are tree-lined walks above the embankments of the Seine.

Parisians and visitors to Paris love to stroll along the quays. A *quay* is a landing place for boats. But the Paris quays are also tree-lined walks and roads above the embankments enclosing the river. (Few people pronounce it *key*, which is the English way. Instead they come as near as they can to the French word, *quai*, giving it a long *a* sound, not an *ee* sound.)

Books and prints line the bookstalls along the Left Bank.

While walking along the quays on the Left Bank, people often stop to look at old books and prints in the bookstalls. These are long wooden boxes clamped to the wall above the embankment. When a sudden shower comes, the covers are closed, but in pleasant weather the bookstalls are open-air bookstores. As many people stop to browse as to buy. Yet walking

27

along the quays must produce an appetite for books, for many are sold. There have been bookstalls on the quays for hundreds of years.

The Cathedral of Notre-Dame is on the Ile de la Cité. The square in front is said to be the geographical center of Paris. The two towers on the west front of the cathedral look strong and solid. Below and between the towers is the great wheel of a stained glass window. The east side of the cathedral has flying buttresses, which are great arches supporting the walls. From a distance in dim light, one can imagine they are oars which almost dip into the Seine. The Palais de Justice is also on the Ile de la

French Government Tourist Office

Right: Grotesque stone gargoyles look down from the towers of Notre-Dame.

Left: The beautiful Cathedral of Notre-Dame was built more than 700 years ago.

French Government Tourist Office

Cité. But the strength and beauty of the great gray cathedral seems to symbolize the best in French civilization.

Paris is a city of gray stone and green trees. It is a city of blue sky and chalk-white clouds, or of silver rain and lavender mist over the river. It is a city of perfume from horse chestnut trees blossoming in April, from lilies of the valley which bring good luck on May Day, from the flower market not far from Notre-Dame. Patient fishermen fish from the embankments and from barges and pleasure boats going up and down the Seine. At night, Paris is a city of shadowy streets and wide, gaily lighted boulevards. It is a city of light—hundreds of quivering lights reflected in the dark water of the river. It is also a city of enlightenment of the mind and of the spirit.

The Seine flows slowly through Paris, as if unwilling to leave the city it has made great and beautiful.

Notre-Dame Cathedral

French Government Tourist Office

At night the quivering lights of Paris are reflected in the river.

3. The Bridges of Paris

A young mother was pushing her baby in a baby carriage over the Pont des Arts, a foot bridge in Paris. Suddenly there was a crash which made the woman fall on her knees. Hastily she got to her feet and hurried the baby carriage the rest of the way across the shaking, sagging bridge.

Then she learned that the mast of a boat towing

31

a 300-ton barge had crashed into an arch of the bridge. The arch had cracked and the bridge was now unsafe. The river was high or the accident might not have happened. If the mast had been lower, it might have cleared the arch. If the boat had been running under sail instead of by motor, the crash might have been less violent. This accident to the Pont des Arts was in January 1960. It is only one of many accidents which have caused Paris bridges to fall down.

There have been bridges over the Seine for many centuries. In the days of the Romans, two stone bridges joined the Ile de la Cité to the Right Bank and the Left. Since then there have been wooden bridges, cast iron bridges and bridges made of steel and stone. Thirty-three bridges now cross the Seine in Paris.

Until after 1800 most of the Paris bridges had shops and houses on them. The buildings were four or five stories high so they cut off a view of the river for people crossing the bridge. Walking or riding by coach or on horseback across the bridge was like

This boat has a sectional smokestack which bends for the low arch of the Pont Alexandre III.

going along a street with a row of houses on either side.

What busy places those old bridges were! There were shops and outdoor markets. In those days a bridge was a combination dwelling place, shopping center and amusement park. Here would be a man selling toys. People stood to watch him make tops

The roadway over an old Paris bridge was jammed with people.

spin, jumping jacks jump and hand puppets bow and wave. Next to him might be a dentist, ready to yank out an aching tooth. A little farther on might be a man with a performing dog or a dancing bear. At times acrobats and tumblers put on shows. Or a rope was stretched across the bridge for tightrope walkers. Jugglers with their bright balls made people stop to watch and to admire and, maybe, to spare a little money for a skilled performance.

"Most delectable pastries for sale. Come buy the beautiful tarts and little cakes," shouted a man who balanced a heavy tray of pastries on his head. Other peddlers sold fish, rabbits, statues of wood or stone— almost anything a person could want to buy. A passer-by could take a fencing lesson, have his por-

Peddlers and entertainers of all kinds did a big business.

Kurt Wiese

trait painted, his knives or sword sharpened, or his hair cut on a Paris bridge long ago before automobiles were even thought of. He might also have his pocket picked, for there were usually petty thieves among the crowd. And beggars held outstretched hands to every kindly face.

The goldsmiths and money changers lived on one bridge. It was devoted to banking and to the making of fine jewelry, golden goblets, and gold and silver tableware which only the nobility could afford to buy. Because money was changed there, the bridge was called the Pont au Change. For generations fine coaches rolled over the bridge. At times a gentleman with a powdered wig, embroidered waistcoat and satin coat and knee breeches would leave his coach

35

Kurt Wiese

Shops and houses lined the two sides of the old Paris bridges.

and enter a shop. He might buy a necklace for some pretty lady of the King's Court.

Of all the Paris bridges, the Pont au Change had the most misfortunes. It is said to have collapsed ten times in 100 years. Houses slid into the river. People were crushed or drowned.

The worst disaster took place at 9:30 on an October evening in the year 1621. A careless servant dropped a lighted candle into some shavings. Wind fanned the flames, and they spread from house to house. All the buildings on the bridge burned, and many lives were lost. Not many people cared to live on that bridge after it was rebuilt.

Not only fires but floods destroyed the bridges. One historian tells how, during an especially high spring flood, a bridge, houses and all, slipped into the river. Nobody was saved except a baby whose cradle floated like a tiny boat.

So many accidents happened to bridges with houses on them that finally a law was passed forbidding buildings on bridges. The Pont Neuf was the first bridge built without houses and shops. It used to have

Fishermen moor their rowboats under the bridges of Paris.

bookstalls. They are no longer on the bridge but on the nearby quays. The Pont Neuf means the *New Bridge*, but it is now the oldest bridge in Paris. It unites the two arms of the Seine at the tip of the Ile de la Cité. Parisians are fond of the Pont Neuf. If an old man is strong and healthy, they say he is as solid as the Pont Neuf. It has lasted, strong and sturdy, since the last part of the sixteenth century.

People have not lived on the bridges of Paris for

a long, long time. But there are still a few who live under the bridges. They are the homeless ones. We would call them hoboes, yet they are a harmless sort. Some of them are old men dressed in ragged clothes. Their long gray hair is tucked under their dirty berets. Often their faces are ruddy and cheerful, as if they enjoy living under a bridge. They sleep on heaps of straw under a stairway leading down to the quay. Or they set up their simple housekeeping under the first arches of a bridge.

If you get up very early, you may see an old man or an old woman pushing a rickety baby carriage toward the Seine. Instead of a baby in the carriage, there will be treasures from trash barrels and even

Kurt Wiese

fruits and vegetables dropped from market trucks. Dwellers under a bridge are sometimes willing to work long enough to get money for a soup bone or a bottle of wine. More often they beg for the money. They seldom look hungry.

It is supposed to be against the law to live under a Paris bridge, but the police are not severe about enforcing the law. A hobo may be told to move on, but it is understood that he may move only to the

Left: A Paris hobo does his laundry by the river. **Below:** These old fellows sleep under one of the bridges at night and spin yarns about the river by day.

Charles Trieschman from Black Star

next bridge. There are not many of these harmless, homeless ones. Often they sleep by day and wander about by night. Of all the people of Paris, they live nearest the Seine.

Most of the bridges of Paris are beautiful. The builders kept in mind that the bridges must be in harmony with palaces, gardens and cathedrals. Some of the bridges are ornamented with stone or bronze sculptures. The Pont Alexandre III is the most ornate. Other bridges are simple in design. The Pont Neuf has the statue of the good King Henri IV in the middle of the bridge.

Traffic is heavy over most of the Paris bridges. Yet people still walk over them. They cross the bridges on foot to get unhurried views of the city and of the river. They walk over a bridge to be refreshed by the sight of the slow, calm river. The people of Paris and their visitors have always enjoyed standing on a Paris bridge to look at the Seine.

4. The Two Patron Saints of Paris

Some countries and a few cities in the world have patron saints. Paris has two, Saint-Denis and Sainte-Geneviève.

Saint-Denis lived at a time when the Romans ruled Paris. Then most of the city was on the Ile de la Cité in the Seine. A pagan altar stood where the Cathedral of Notre-Dame now stands. Yet there were already a few Christians in Paris. And in the year

252 Bishop Denis was sent from Rome to convert more people to Christianity.

The Romans did not want the people in Paris to become Christians. They wanted them to worship the Roman gods. Saint-Denis was ordered to stop holding meetings for Christians, but he would not obey. The meetings continued in secret. Sometimes the early Christians met in caves where stone had been quarried under the Left Bank.

The Romans found out about these secret meetings. A law was passed proclaiming that anyone caught preaching Christianity would be put to death.

Bishop Denis did not want to die, but he was sure it was his duty to go on preaching. For several years he managed to work in secret. But one day Roman soldiers learned of a meeting and arrested him and several of his followers. They were brought before a judge and sentenced to death. They were beheaded on a high hill on the outskirts of Paris. Later the hill was named Montmartre, meaning the *Hill of Martyrs*.

There is a legend that as soon as the head of Saint-Denis was struck off, he stooped and picked it up.

Inside the Church of Saint-Denis.

Then with his severed head under his arm, he walked for miles. Finally he sank lifeless at the spot where he wished to be buried.

Long ago Frenchmen went into battle shouting, "Forward for Saint-Denis!" Denis is remembered today by the industrial suburb of Paris called Saint-Denis. There is a Church of Saint-Denis, too, where kings and queens of France have been buried. The name of the good bishop was also given to a canal which provides power for industry in Paris. The name of Saint-Denis lives on.

There is no canal of the Seine named after Sainte-Geneviève, the other patron saint of Paris. But she, too, is remembered with affection. As a young girl Geneviève came to Paris from a nearby village. She soon gained the reputation of being a devout Christian. This was a time when hordes of Huns, led by the fierce warrior, Attila, were invading Europe. Attila advanced almost to Paris, and the Parisians were terrified. Geneviève prayed that the Huns would bypass Paris, and they did. The people believed that her prayers saved the city from invasion.

Then there came a time when Paris was besieged. Enemy tribes controlled the Seine both above and below Paris. Since the Seine was the chief highway, the people of Paris would starve if food could not be brought in by boat. Boats had tried to get out of Paris but were captured.

Then Geneviève chose brave, strong men to try again. One night, with muffled oars they rowed a boat out of the city and up the river. As if in answer to prayer, a heavy mist hid them. They reached the city of Troyes in safety and loaded their boat with wheat. Again the dark, the mist and their confidence in the prayers of Geneviève helped them. They arrived safely at Paris, and the city then had bread.

The people of Paris named a hill on the Left Bank for Geneviève. They planned to make the Panthéon her church. But it became a temple to glorify famous Frenchmen. Yet not many people come to the Panthéon to see the tombs of famous men. Instead they come to see the wall paintings which tell the story of Sainte-Geneviève. The favorite scene shows her standing on a high balcony looking down at the city. There is a moon high in the sky, and below is all of Paris with the river at its heart.

Geneviève seems to stand guard over the city and to protect it. Some think she is the guardian angel of Paris.

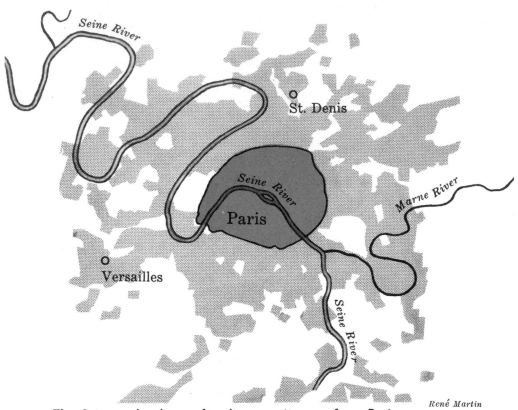

René Martin

The Seine makes loop after loop on its way from Paris.

5. Chalk Hills and a Castle

From Paris the Seine goes on its winding way toward the English Channel. There are bends in the river before it reaches Paris. A twisty part of the river is in the very center of the city. But the deepest loops are after the Seine leaves Paris. One loop after another is like a big capital S. It is as if the Seine kept writing its initial letter on the countryside. Frenchmen give a joking reason why the Seine has so many loops. They say the river is so beautiful that it keeps coming back to admire itself. But we know there are hills which the lower Seine must go around. And the slope of the land is very gentle.

The Seine is very dirty as it flows through the industrial suburbs of Paris. Much of the waste from the factories goes into the canals of Saint-Denis and Saint-Martin. The French government is working to make the Seine cleaner in and around Paris, but there is still too much waste and sewage going into the river.

On a loop of the Seine at the very edge of Paris, is the town of Sèvres. Almost everybody in town works in the china factory. Sèvres china used to be made only for the royalty and nobility. Now anybody can buy it. Sèvres china is beautiful but expensive. The bridge over the river at Sèvres is often spoken of as the china bridge although it is made of steel.

From Sèvres, the Seine begins a loop which passes through the suburbs which are the machine shops of

A worker in the
china factory
in Sèvres.

Paris. From them come automobiles, airplanes, paper
and many other manufactured articles. There is much
soot and smoke. In spite of the smoke, however, now
and then there are gardens and orchards. Fruit trees
are trained to grow on walls like vines. The suburbs
used to furnish the Paris market with most of its fruit
and vegetables. Now the factories have crowded out
many of the gardens.

Ten miles from Paris another loop of the river en-
closes the forest of Saint-Germain. Kings and nobles

50

used to hunt in the forest, which is now more park than woods. A beautiful terrace overlooks the river and seems far away from the nearby industrial towns of Asnières, Clichy, and Saint-Denis. But industry is necessary. The busy factories on the outskirts of Paris make it an important manufacturing center.

The Seine leaves the industrial suburbs of Paris and continues its northwestward journey. At the town of Conflans, the Seine is joined at the right by another big river, the Oise. Conflans is a busy barge depot,

This is a black-and-white print of the colorful painting by Alfred Sisley which he called "The Banks of the Oise."

National Gallery of Art, Washington, D. C. (Chester Dale Collection)

At Etretat, these chalk cliffs rise from the English Channel near the mouth of the river Seine.

where barges stop to be refueled. But the bargemen, except for eating and drinking in the riverside restaurants, live on their barges. On Sundays the bargemen and their families even attend church on a barge.

Soon after the Oise joins the Seine, there is a change in the landscape. No longer does the river flow over a limestone bed. Now it flows over chalk. All this part of France has a chalk foundation and is known as the chalk country. Instead of going around all the hills,

Above Le Havre, you can see patches of white chalk in the hills along the river. This is the view from the Château-Gaillard.

the Seine slices through some of them. From the river bank rise hills showing patches of white chalk. Hills hundreds of feet high are topped with grass and trees. In some of the chalk cliffs there are caves with people living in them. There is even an underground church with only the steeple showing. In times of war the chalk caves have been good hiding places.

A mile down river from the underground church, the Château-Gaillard overlooks the Seine. (*Château* is the French word for *castle*.) It is perched like a fortress high on a chalk cliff. The castle was built for the English king, Richard the Lion-Hearted, at the end of the twelfth century. At that time both England and France claimed that part of France. The English held it, and the French were fighting to regain it.

When the castle was finished, King Richard is supposed to have said, "Here is a gallant castle."

The French king said, "Were that castle made of iron, I shall take it."

King Richard's reply to that boast was, "Had it been made of butter, I would still defend the castle against him and his."

The castle remained in the hands of the English while King Richard lived. After his death, it was captured by the French. During the next 200 years it kept changing hands. Part of the time it was held by the French, and part of the time by the English. Then in 1449 the English left France, and no French territory has been under English rule since that time.

But the Château-Gaillard was seldom a peaceful castle. For a time a band of river pirates made it their headquarters. On dark nights the pirates went out from the château to attack barges heading down river to the coast or up river to Paris. Rich cargoes were stolen. Bargemen and their families were killed and drowned. There were rumors of dreadful deeds done behind the thick walls of the castle. Bargemen were

From the river you see the ruins of the Château-Gaillard.

French Government Tourist Office

afraid to pass the castle at night, for fear of pirates lying in wait for them. The pirates would come in their swift rowboats, their oars muffled. They would be cruel and without mercy.

Many French police lost their lives trying to capture the river pirates, for the Château-Gaillard was easy to defend. Finally the French government had the castle destroyed. But enough of the château remains to show how fine it used to be.

There are other castles along the Seine. None looks so much like a storybook castle as the Château-Gaillard, even in its ruins.

Chalk cliffs at Etretat on the English Channel near the Seine.

6. The Hill of the Two Lovers

Some of the chalk hills along the Seine slope gently to the river's edge. In places, however, the river has cut so deep through the chalk hills, that one can see layer after layer of chalk. From these layers you can get a general idea of the age of the Seine. Geologists tell us it took thousands of years to cut through each layer.

One hill near the Seine has an old legend. It seems that many years ago there lived a haughty nobleman who had a beautiful daughter. One day she went for a walk in the woods near her father's home. Suddenly a wild boar ran toward her. Its mean pig-eyes were angry. Its tusks were ready to tear her tender flesh.

The girl screamed. A young peasant, out gathering wood, heard her cry. Bravely he struck at the wild boar with his axe and finally killed it.

The nobleman's daughter was grateful to the young peasant for saving her life. He was strong and brave and handsome. She was pretty, plump and pleasant. They fell in love.

The young peasant went to the nobleman and asked to marry his daughter. And the girl pleaded with her father to let the marriage take place.

But the nobleman was proud. He did not want his daughter to marry a peasant. He refused to let them be married, but his daughter gave him no peace. She pleaded, wept and swore that she would never marry unless she could marry the man she loved. At last the girl's father agreed that they could marry if the young man could pass a test of strength. Not far from the river a steep hillside rose to a height of 600 feet. The test was that the young man should carry the girl to the top of the hill without stopping or letting her fall.

All the neighborhood came to see the young peasant try to win his bride. They saw him take the pretty plump girl in his strong arms. They cheered as he started on a run up the steep hillside.

Soon his run slowed to a walk. His breathing grew labored. Cold sweat was on his forehead.

"Keep on, my dear one. Do not let me fall," the nobleman's daughter kept saying to him.

Putting forth a supreme effort, the young man reached the top of the steep hill. A cheer went up from those watching below. The peasant had proved his strength. Now he could marry the nobleman's daughter. Everybody, except perhaps the nobleman, was happy for him.

But the happiness did not last. As the young man set the girl on her feet, he fell dead. His heart had not been able to stand the strain.

The nobleman's daughter was so grieved that she leaped into the Seine and was drowned. And since that day the hill where all this took place has been known as Le Côte des Deux Amants, *The Hill of the Two Lovers.*

There is a happier version of this legend. In this one, the young man only fainted. Then the two lovers were married and lived happily ever after.

7. Factory Chimneys and
Church Steeples

It is 87 miles by train from Paris to the city of
Rouen. By boat, the trip is much longer because of the
many loops of the Seine. The banks of the river are
not all chalk cliffs. There are stretches where the hills
stand back a mile or more from the river. Then come
miles where the river bank is high on one side and low

and marshy on the other. The scenery is so varied that if the river could speak it might say, "If you don't like this kind of scenery, go on a little farther and it will be different."

From Paris to Rouen the Seine is busier than it is above Paris. Tugs pull longer strings of barges. More factory chimneys appear among the church spires of the towns.

No two towns are alike. Mantes has beaches of white sand. Vernon is on the one straight length of river between Paris and Rouen. Les Andelys slopes down to the river, with outcroppings of chalk showing. The river towns are pretty, with many trees. Here, as along the upper Seine, there are willows, lime trees, plane trees, oaks, and most frequent of all, poplars.

Between the towns on the Seine from Paris to Rouen, there are miles of woods and farm land. Fat cattle feed contentedly in the meadows. Sweet yellow plums and ruddy pears and apples grow against sunny walls or in pleasant orchards. Here and there are outcroppings of chalk as tall as factory chimneys, and one is seldom out of sight of the hills.

The lower Seine is dotted with islands. They are long, narrow strips of woods or meadow. The longest island is eight miles long. Men come in rowboats to fish or a family for a picnic. River pirates used to have their strongholds on some of the islands, which are so peaceful today.

When the Seine reaches the town of Elbeuf, the rural look of the landscape disappears. Elbeuf, on a southern loop of the river, bristles with factory chimneys. It is a town of woolen mills, cotton mills and dye works. There are factories for making soap and hosiery.

Rouen is on the next loop of the river. A few miles above Rouen the first influence of the tide is felt. Here the sea begins mingling with the river water. It is 55 miles by land from Rouen to the seaport of Le Havre at the mouth of the Seine. By boat the distance is more than twice as far. That is because the Seine makes two great loops between Rouen and the English Channel.

The city of Rouen is about midway between Paris and the sea. There the river is deep enough for large boats that cannot go up river to Paris. Heavier and larger ships need deep water to keep afloat. Ships drawing 20 feet of water can dock at Rouen. Those coming from the English Channel which are too large to go beyond Rouen shift their cargoes to smaller boats which go to Paris. And barges coming from Paris reload their cargoes on larger vessels. These go on to Le Havre, at the mouth of the Seine, or to foreign ports. Rouen is sometimes called the port of Paris.

Along the busy waterfront, cranes and derricks load

From Paris to the Channel, the Seine takes a winding route.

René Martin

ENGLISH CHANNEL

F R A N C E

Le Havre

Honfleur

Rouen

Risle River

Elbeuf

Les Andelys

Eure River

Vernon

Oise River

Seine River

St. Denis

The Seine
Downriver from Paris

Paris

and unload freighters from Sweden and Norway. Tankers take on oil. Wine, lumber and cattle are loaded on ships bound for far ports. Yet the deep whistles of ocean ships do not sound as often as the impatient toots of the river tugs. Long strings of barges constantly arrive and leave the docks of Rouen. A network of canals connecting the Seine with other rivers comes together here, bearing goods for Paris or from Paris. Rouen handles more river traffic than any port of France.

This is a very old city. Some historians claim it is older than Paris. Rouen was the ancient capital of Normandy when that province was ruled by a duke. In those days France was not a united country but was made up of dukedoms. William the Conqueror was the most famous duke of Normandy. He took troops across the English Channel and conquered England in the year 1066. Then he became King of England as well as Duke of Normandy. He lived for years in England, but he died at Rouen.

Someone much dearer to the hearts of the French people than William the Conqueror died at Rouen.

Right: Ancient houses on a narrow street of Rouen.

French Government Tourist Office

Statue of Jeanne d'Arc in the old market place of Rouen.

Their national heroine, Jeanne d'Arc, was convicted
of witchcraft and was burned at the stake there in the
year 1431. Clad in armor, she had led troops in vic-

The Cathedral of Rouen.

French Government Tourist Office

torious battles against the English. Her love for
France shone in all her deeds. Her statue in the old
market place of Rouen is visited like a shrine.

67

Rouen is a many-steepled city. Although it is a busy industrial town, it has more church spires than factory chimneys. The great cathedral of Rouen and many other churches were damaged by bombs during World War II. But the fourteenth-century church of Saint-Ouen was unharmed, although it has one of the highest steeples. A great clock on a high tower has told time since the fifteenth century.

Damage by war is nothing new to Rouen. Norsemen invaded the town in the ninth century. Before the last half of the fifteenth century, the city was held several times by the English. It has been many years since the English occupied Rouen. Yet three times during the past hundred years the Germans have captured the city.

The damage done in World War II is still being repaired. Shattered docks have been rebuilt. New factories hum with industry. One of the bridges across the Seine has an electric moving platform to carry people across the river. In Rouen, the new and the modern blend with the old.

After every war, Rouen has always set to work to

rebuild the city. No enemy can destroy the reason for Rouen's importance: its position on the Seine. Because France needs a port halfway between Paris and the sea, Rouen has endured through the ages.

Barges, river boats and ocean-going vessels unload at Rouen.

8. On to Le Havre

The town of Duclair is on the top of the next loop of the Seine, down river from Rouen. Duclair is only seven miles by land from Rouen but over 22 miles by river.

The Seine makes another even larger loop before it reaches the seaport of Le Havre. Between Rouen and Le Havre there are dikes on each side of the Seine. These man-made embankments narrow the river, making it deeper and swifter. Rows of poplar trees have been planted on land which used to be river bottom. Vegetables are raised on this made land, and fat cattle stand in the meadows. Here the Seine is a wide, majestic river even though it has been narrowed by dikes.

From Rouen on, the tide grows stronger. More water rushes in from the sea. But even at the last stage of its long journey, the Seine's current is strong. Almost at the mouth, the river Risle joins the Seine. This is the last of the many tributaries which pour their waters into the Seine. Some of the tributaries are larger than the river they join. But they all become part of the Seine. It is like the trunk of a tree with the tributaries its branches.

As the Seine nears its mouth, it becomes wider. Sand bars appear in midstream. Dredges work to keep the river free of silt. But the force of the river current and the rush of the incoming tide cause sand bars to shift and new ones to form.

Here the Seine is no longer a placid stream. When the strong river current meets the incoming tide, the water is especially rough and turbulent. Because of the rough water and the shifting sand bars, most boats need a pilot to take them safely along this part of the Seine. Those who know the river well can avoid the shallows. They know when to take a ship close to the river bank to keep from being caught in the bore.

A bore is a tidal wave in a river. It is caused when a strong river current meets an incoming tide at its full. As it flows downstream, the Seine's current is strong. It is so strong that it slows the tide coming in from the sea. Tidal waters pile up. It is as if the river were holding back the sea. But at flood tide the sea wins. The water spills over into a great wave that sweeps up river. The bore is highest when the tide is highest. In the spring when there is a new moon, the tide is especially high. The bore in the Seine may reach a height of 10 feet or more.

The force of the bore is hardly felt as far up river as Rouen. Farther downstream at the town of Quillebeuf, the bore at high tide in the spring is spectacular. There the river is only three-quarters of a mile wide. The current is swift and the water deep.

People drive from as far away as Rouen to see the bore at Quillebeuf in the spring. They can hear the bore before they can see it. From a distance it sounds like an approaching freight train, coming at full speed. Then comes the great crested wave sweeping up river. As it travels up river, the bore gradually flattens and is lost in the river. At its height, it is beautiful. The bore of the Seine is not huge enough to be frightening. But it is safer for small boats to stay out of its way at a high spring tide.

There is good fishing after the Seine feels the influence of the tides. The fresh water begins to be brackish with salt water as far up river as Rouen. Yet there are fresh-water smelts and crayfish for miles after the river becomes tidal. Fresh-water fish can stand a certain amount of salt in the water.

At the mouth of the Seine there is salt-water fishing, less fishing for sport and more commercial fishing. Fishing boats go out after lobsters and large crayfish, which are like lobsters without their large pincers.

The Seine flings its arms wide to meet the English

Lobster traps on a French dock.

The old town of Honfleur was once the seaport of the Seine.

Channel. The two river banks form a V. Between the banks is the estuary or mouth of the Seine. Before the arms swing out, a canal at the town of Tancarville takes river traffic to and from Le Havre. Thus small boats can avoid the rougher water of the estuary.

On the left of the estuary is the old town of Honfleur. It used to be the seaport of the Seine. But

French Government Tourist Office

Ocean liners and freighters crowd the harbor of Le Havre.

there were many shifting sand bars at Honfleur. So the city of Le Havre was built on the right of the estuary to handle ocean and river traffic. Now Honfleur is a port mostly for fishermen.

Although newer than Honfleur, Le Havre began to be an important seaport by the end of the sixteenth century. Like Rouen, the city has suffered from many wars. Yet it has always been rebuilt. It has docks for ocean liners, and its waterfront is busy with the loading and unloading of freighters. Ships are built in the shipyards, and machine shops hum and clang. Le Havre is one of the entrances to France. It has a direct steamship route to New York.

At Le Havre, the Seine reaches its destination and empties into the English Channel. This is the end of the river road that comes from the heart of France.

This new bridge across the Seine is 1,994 feet long.

French Government Tourist Office

Kurt Wiese

9. The Pictured River

Few rivers in the world have inspired half as much art as the Seine. Certainly the river is partly responsible for making Paris a great art center.

Early French artists, to be sure, did not paint pictures of the Seine. Their pictures were of battles, of gods and goddesses, or of people. If the river did appear, it was an unimportant part of the landscape.

Then the artist Courbet decided he did not want to paint pictures that told stories. He set up his easel outdoors and painted trees, rocks and rivers as he saw them. In the year 1856, he painted the picture, "Girls on the Banks of the Seine." In this picture, the Seine is the important part, not just background.

Courbet loved nature. Some people say he brought French painting outdoors.

Another French artist who was a great nature lover was Corot. For many years he lived just outside Paris. He painted lovely misty landscapes in cool greens and grays. The Seine appears in some of his pictures, but he is best known for his painting of trees. There is a springtime look about many of his pictures.

Corot's pictures sold well during his lifetime. In the year 1871 Corot gave $10,000 to help the poor in Paris. That was a lot of money then. Corot was over 70 years old when he made his gift to the poor of Paris. He remembered when he had been poor. Now that he was rich, he wanted to share his good fortune.

One morning in the year 1878, a shabbily dressed man entered the shop of a Paris art dealer. Under each arm he carried several unframed oil paintings.

The art dealer looked at each painting. "Very pretty, Monsieur Sisley," he said. "You have talent. But why do you always paint river scenes? You paint pictures of the river Seine—the river Loing—always rivers. And there's little market for river pic-

A black-and-white print of a colorful river painting by Corot.

tures, especially for the kind you paint. You must agree that a picture of yours looks best when viewed from a distance."

"What I paint I see from a distance," argued the artist. "And Corot has painted river scenes. His pictures bring good prices."

"True. True," agreed the art dealer. "I can sell a

Corot. But I remember when his pictures did not find buyers. Be patient. Perhaps in time your river pictures will become the fashion."

"My wife and children find it difficult to wait for that time," said Sisley. "I have a family to provide for, you understand. You say I have talent. Then advance me enough money to feed my family for six months. In exchange, you shall have twenty of my best paintings. You may have your choice."

The art dealer shook his head. "I regret. I greatly regret, Monsieur Sisley, but I cannot pay you for your paintings. I could not sell them."

Sisley left the shop, carrying his unwanted paintings. He must have been very discouraged. Once more he had to go home without having sold a picture. Sisley lived at Moret, near where the river Loing joins the Seine. He painted many pictures both of the Seine and of the Loing. Although he seldom sold a picture and was very poor, he kept on painting river scenes. He could not afford to buy leather shoes so he wore wooden shoes. But he went on painting the kind of pictures he wanted to paint.

Sisley painted rivers in all seasons and in every kind of weather. He painted the river as a mirror of the sky in sunlight and in mist. Not many of his paintings sold until after his death. Then they suddenly became famous. Soon one picture would sell for more than he had asked the art dealer for twenty. But one cannot feel too sorry for Sisley. He was poor all his life, but he did what he most enjoyed doing. He painted river scenes because he loved to paint them.

A friend of Sisley's was the artist Monet. He also

With soft greens, yellows and blues, Monet painted "The Banks of the Seine," shown here in black and white.

loved rivers. He painted 18 pictures of the same part of the Seine. Each picture was different, for each was painted at a different time of day or in different weather. Some of his paintings show only sky and water and reeds along the river bank. In others there are views of a bridge, of fishermen, or of boats on the Seine. Like Sisley, he did beautiful pictures of reflections in the water. He is most famous for his skill in painting sunlight on the river. Some people think he is still the most successful painter of sunshine.

Since Monet and Sisley, many artists have painted pictures of the Seine. In good weather there are always easels set up on the Paris quays. Artists busily paint what they see. Or they try to paint what they feel about what they see.

Photographers, too, make pictures of the river. Truly the Seine is a much-pictured river.

10. The Moving Road

The Seine is naturally a good highway. It is slow and steady until it nears its mouth. It has no deep gorges or swift rapids. Except for a few miles at its beginning, boats can travel its entire length. Even its many loops are like curves in a well-planned road.

Ocean liners leave and arrive at Le Havre, and big oil tankers are at the docks of Rouen. More characteristic of the Seine are the barges. Long before the time of railroads, trucks and planes, traffic by barge had made Paris one of the great trade centers of the world. There are still many barges on the Seine.

Years ago the barges had to be rowed or sailed. Now a barge may have an engine and travel alone. Or it may be engineless and be one of a long line of barges towed by a tugboat.

There is something quite cozy-looking about some of the Seine barges. Many of them are over 100 feet long. There are holds for cargo at each end and cabin space between the holds. Often curtains trim the cabin windows, and window boxes are bright with flowers. Clothes flap from lines hung across the deck. Sometimes small children may be seen playing on deck.

A city as large as Paris needs to have many tons of food and merchandise brought in every day. Years ago, barges brought wheat, oats, wine, salt, herring, bacon, honey, butter, cheese, tin, iron, fruit, nuts, wool, hides, copper, brass, hemp, linen, silk and many other products. Trucks and freight trains carry the bulk of these products now. Most of the barges bound for Paris carry cement, oil, coal, wood and other freight not needed in a hurry.

Freight has always gone out of Paris as well as

The barge, *Jeanne d'Arc,* is owned by the captain who lives aboard. Here you see his granddaughter who has spent most of her life on the barge, going up and down the river Seine.

Curtains trim the windows of this Seine River boat.

coming into the city. For hundreds of years Paris shipped perfume, hats, dresses, rugs and carpets, glassware, china, jewelry, fine leather goods and other luxury items. They went in barges to the coast. There they were loaded on larger ships. The label "Made in Paris" was known all over the world.

Paris merchandise still goes all over the world. But not so much is carried in the holds of barges. Yet shipping on the Seine has been increasing in the past few years. Barges give the slowest and the cheapest form of transportation. Nowadays the holds of barges may be filled with bottles of wine or crates of machinery. But the time may come when Seine barges may smell of perfume again instead of oil.

Highways must be improved from time to time. So must rivers. The Seine has been widened where it is deep and more width is needed. It has been narrowed to make it deep enough for large boats, especially near the sea.

In many parts of the river, dams have been built to furnish water power for factories. Locks have been constructed to help river traffic. A lock in a river is like a staircase in a building. It raises or lowers the level of the river.

Suppose you are going up the Seine, and you come to a lock. A gate opens, and your boat comes in at downstream level. The gate closes, and your boat is enclosed by damp stone walls. Water is let in to raise your boat until it comes out at a higher level. Locks govern the level of the river. They are needed at many

Photo from European

River barges are towed in long trains by powerful tugboats. These tugs are waiting at the fuel station for further loads.

shallow spots in the Seine. There are eight locks upstream from Paris and nine from Paris to the sea.

Besides dams and locks, the Seine has many canals. Some canals are built to relieve the main stream from traffic, as the canals Saint-Denis and Saint-Martin at Paris. Other canals have been made to connect the Seine with other rivers. A network of canals links the Seine and its tributaries to the eastern and

Beyond Notre-Dame Cathedral, you see the Seine in working clothes. Here a steam shovel is unloading gravel from a barge. *Below:* Covered barges are waiting to be unloaded.

northern parts of France and to Germany and Belgium. These canals have greatly expanded the trade of Paris, for barges can travel by water far into France and to Germany. The canals are like connecting roads between highways. Or they are waterways to give towns and villages a route to the Seine.

Until the seventeenth century, canals and locks were built by local communities. Now they are under the control of the French government, for the Seine

A typical Seine River boat with smokestack that can be lowered.

Photo from European

is of national importance. With so many other means of transportation today, the Seine is not the only highway to be improved. Yet it is still an important road to and from Paris.

There are larger rivers in the world than the Seine. But this river has been important in the history of Europe. The Seine has mirrored battles and revolutions. It has inspired artists and authors. It has been praised in song and in verse.

The Seine is a useful river, too. It feeds the hungry with its abundant fish. Its water power keeps the wheels of industry turning. And its moving waters carry cargoes over most of France and beyond France.

The Seine is a famous river because Paris, cultural center of the world, had its beginning on an island in the river. When people speak of the banks of the Seine, they often mean Paris. But the Seine is more than Paris.

It is the washerwomen rinsing their clothes in the running stream, the fishermen casting their lines into quiet depths, the little river towns with their main street on the riverside and the busier towns with their mills and docks and spires. It is the boats—house-boats, rowboats, tugboats, tankers, sailboats and, most of all, the barges. The Seine is all of these.

The river is a mirror of crinkled glass in the morning breeze and of stained glass of many colors in the sunset. It is home to the river birds, to the ducks, to the fish. It is a river that belongs to the many people who love it. It is Paris and more than Paris. It is THE SEINE.

A spring scene on the Left Bank.

Photo from European

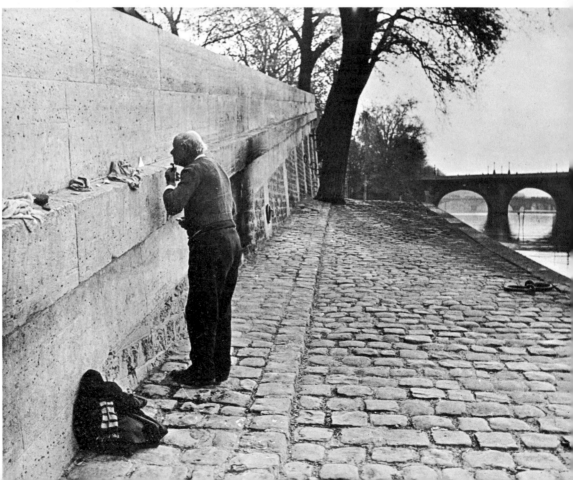

Pronunciation Guide

This list will make it easier for you to pronounce the French words in this book. The sound of "jh" is the same as "s" in the word "measure." To say the "ü," set your lips as if you were going to whistle.

Aube River	ōb
Château-Gaillard	shǎ–to' gǎ–yǎr'
Conflans	kōn–flǎn'
Corot	kō–rō'
La Côte des Deux Amants	lah coat deh duh zah–mahn'
Côte-d'Or	coat door'
Courbet	koor–bě'
Dieppe	dē–yěp'
Douix River	doo–ē'
Duclair	dü–klare'
Elbeuf	el–buff'
Etretat	ā–tr–tah'
Honfleur	ŏn–flurr'
Ile de la Cité	eel' duh lah see–teh'
Ile Saint-Louis	eel' san–loo–ee'
Jeanne d'Arc	jhan dark
Le Havre	luh ǎ'vr
Les Andelys	leh zahn–d'lē'
Loing River	loo–an'
Louvre	loo'vr
Mantes	mahnt
Monet	mō–ně'
Montereau	mohn–trō'
Montmartre	mohn–mǎr'tr
Montparnasse	mohn–pǎr–nahs'
Nogent	nō–jhan'
Oise River	wahz
Palais de Justice	pah–leh duh jhews–tiss
Panthéon	pahn–tě–ohn
Pont Alexandre III	pōn al–ex–zan'dr twa
Pont au Change	pōn oh shanzh'
Pont des Arts	pōn deh zaar'
Pont Neuf	pōn nuf'
Quillebeuf	kē–yē–buff'
Risle River	reel
Rouen	roo–ahn'
Sacré-Coeur	sak'ray kerr
Saint-Denis	sahn d'nee'
Sainte-Geneviève	sahnt jhan'v–ev
Saint-Germain	sahn zher–mǎn'
Saint-Mammès	sahn mah–mess
Saint-Ouen	sahn twan'
Sèvres	seh'vr
Troyes	twah
Utrillo	ü–trē'yo
Vernon	věr–nohn'
Yonne River	yawn

Index

Agriculture, 15, 50, 61, 70
　Vineyards, 8
Aube River, 14

Barges, 13, 14, 32, 51–52, 55,
　61, 63, 64, 83–87, 88, 89,
　92
Bookstalls, 27, 29
Bridges, 76
　Paris, 31–42

Canals, 46, 49, 64, 74, 88–90
Chalk country, 52–54, 56, 57,
　60, 61
　Legend, 57–59
Château-Gaillard, 53–56
China industry, 49–50
Christianity, 43–44, 46–47
Conflans, 51–52
Corot, Jean Baptiste, 78, 79
Côte des Deux Amants, Le,
　57–59
Côte-d'Or, 8
Courbet, Gustave, 77–78

Dams and locks, 87–88, 90
Dieppe, endsheets
Dikes, 70
Douix River, 13
Duclair, 70

Eiffel Tower, 24, 25
Elbeuf, 62
English Channel, 17, 62, 63,
　64, 73–74
English in France, 54, 68
Etretat, 52, 56

Fishing, 5, 12–13, 15, 16, 17,
　30, 38, 73, 75, 91
France (map), 6

Germans in France, 68

Hill of the Two Lovers, 57–59
Hoboes, 39–42
Honfleur, 74–75
Huns, 46

Ile de la Cité,
　See Paris
Ile Saint-Louis,
　See Paris
Industry, 14, 49–50, 51, 61,
　62, 68, 76

Jeanne d'Arc, 66–67
Joan of Arc,
　See Jeanne d'Arc

Laundries, Outdoor, 10, 40, 91
Left Bank,
　See Paris

Le Havre, 75–76, 83
Les Andelys, 61
Loing River, 80
Louvre, 22
Lutetia, 19
Luxembourg Gardens, 22–24

Mantes, 61
Marne River, 16
Monet, Claude, 81–82
Montereau, 14, 15

Nogent, 14
Normandy, 64
Norsemen in France, 21–22, 68
Notre-Dame, Cathedral of, 25, 28–30, 43

Ocean-going vessels, 62–64, 76, 83
Oise River, 51–52

Palais de Justice, 29–30
Panthéon, 24, 47
Paris, 7, 17, 18–30, 48–49, 91, 92
  Bridges, 31–42
  History, 19–21
  Ile de la Cité, 18–19, 22, 25, 29–30, 32, 38, 43
  Ile Saint-Louis, 18–19, 22, 25
  Left Bank, 22–24, 25, 27–29, 31, 44, 47, 92
  Map, 48
  Montmartre, 22, 23, 25, 44

Montparnasse, 25
Motto, 20–21
Patron saints, 43–47
Right Bank, 22, 25, 31
Seal, 20
Suburbs, 49–51
Pirates, 54–56, 62
Pont Alexandre III, 32, 42
Pont au Change, 35–37
Pont des Arts, 31–32
Pont Neuf, 37–38, 42

Quays, 26–29
Quillebeuf, 72

Richard I (the Lion-Hearted), King of England, 54
Right Bank,
  See Paris
Risle River, 71
River boats, 31–32, 33, 63, 71
Romans in France, 9, 19, 43–44
Rouen, 62–69, 72, 73, 83
Rouen, Cathedral of, 67, 68

Sacré-Coeur, 23, 25
Saint-Denis, 43–46
Saint-Denis (canal), 46, 49, 88
Saint-Denis (church), 45
Saint-Denis (suburb of Paris), 45, 51
Sainte-Geneviève, 43, 46–47

Saint-Germain, 50–51
Saint-Mammès, 14
Saint-Ouen, Church of, 68
Seine River
  Artistic inspiration, 77–82
  Bridges, 31–42, 76
  Estuary, 74–76
  Floods, 11, 37
  Islands, 62
  Lower Seine, 52–57, 60–73
  Maps,
    France, 6
    Lower Seine, 63
    Paris, 48
    Upper Seine, 11
  Paris, 17–30, 48–49
  Source, 8–9

Tide, 62, 71–73
Transportation, 83–91
Upper Seine, 8–17
Sequana, 9
Sèvres, 49–50
Sisley, Alfred, 51, 78–81, 82

Trade and commerce, 19, 20,
  63–64, 83–87
Troyes, 13–14, 47

Utrillo, Maurice, 23

Vernon, 61

William I (the Conqueror),
  King of England, 64

Yonne River, 14, 15

Meet the Author

HAZEL WILSON was born in Portland, Maine, but she has lived many years in Washington, D. C. She is a former librarian and for a number of years has taught Children's Literature at George Washington University. She is the author of 15 books for young readers. *The Seine* is her third book with a French background.

For over two years, Mrs. Wilson lived in Paris where she worked at the American Library. While in Paris, she developed a great love of the Seine River. She took boat trips up and down the river in the days when excursion boats went farther than they do today. On pleasant Sundays she often rambled along the quays and walked over bridges between the Right and Left Bank and those connecting the Ile de la Cité with the mainland.

"Some of the beauty of the Seine is beyond description," says Mrs. Wilson, "but I have tried to put into words what I feel and know about this beautiful river."

The Seine in Paris

Air France